31 Days of Praying for Yourself

Speak from your Heart to the Father, Son and Holy Spirit

Abolade Alabi Durojaiye

Scripture from the New Kings James Version

I hope this prayer book
awakens your spirit and inspires you to speak to God freely.

From my heart to yours,

BeBe
Be who God created you to **Be**

This book is dedicated to my Husband, Children and Fellow Sojourners

My Husband:
Darling Dpop, thank you for helping me go deeper with God. You are a God chaser and I love you for this and so much more. May our journey and union bless generations and strengthen marriages to the glory of His name. Amen.

My Children:
Eyitemi Daniel, Similoluwa David and Dideoluwa Deborah, my precious hearts, my pompoms, life is richer because of you. My total dependence on God aids the enormous responsibility to train you up and plant your feet in His footsteps. I pray that you never let go of Gods hand. Continue to abide in Him as He abides in You. Amen. I love you extraordinarily.

My Fellow Sojourners:
Our journey is for a purpose greater than ourselves and we will finish strong, if we stay the course. Do not go it alone. Choose to walk with God. Talk to Him everywhere and at anytime. We should not make prayer complicated. Speak simply, freely and openly. He hears us when we call.

CONTENTS

Introduction: Total Dependence

Day 1: Surrender

Day 2: Your Path for me

Day 3: Your Image of me

Day 4: My Father's Business.

Day 5: Good Success

Day 6: Secret Sin

Day 7: Forgive like You

Day 8: Brother's Keeper

Day 9: Parents

Day 10: Siblings and Extended Family

Day 11: Friends

Day 12: Career

Day 13: Teachers

Day 14: Spouse

Day 15: Children

Day 16: Like Joseph

Day 17: My Place

Day 18: Money

Day 19: The Actual Church

Day 20: Broken Heart

Day 21: Good Works

Day 22: Hopelessness

Day 23: Darkness

Day 24: My Heart

Day 25: My Calling

Day 26: My Home

Day 27: Go with Me

Day 28: Dreams

Day 29: Perilous Pestilence

Day 30: Abundance

Day 31: Just Reward

Names of God

Final Note: Give Up, Give In and Surrender All

Acknowledgements

INTRODUCTION

Total Dependence

Life is not easy but it is beautiful, when God is your anchor. I talk to God like I am having a normal conversation. I talk to Him everywhere and sometimes have to use my headpiece, so I do not appear crazy to others. He gives me perfect answers, all the time. His instructions aren't always easy to follow. Especially when the answer I want is not the one I receive. However, when I obey His instructions, I find peace and joy, no matter the circumstance.

Prayer is not supposed to be complicated, but it can certainly become a chore and something you avoid if you make it complicated. It should not be a badge of spirituality or superiority. Do not be discouraged because you do not sound "holy," and cannot use religious jargon. Do not let anything prevent you from praying. Use your own words to speak Gods words back to Him.

God listens when we speak. He gave us a perfect example of how to pray in the "Lords Prayer."

Mathew 6:9-13

9. In this manner, therefore, pray
Our Father in heaven
Hallowed be Your name.
10. _Your Kingdom_ come
Your will be done
On earth as it is in heaven
11. _Give us_ this day our daily bread
12. And _forgive us_ our debts,
As we forgive our debtors.
13. And _do not lead_ us into temptation,
But _deliver us_ from the evil one.
for Yours is the kingdom, and the Power,
and the glory forever, Amen.

The more I recited these words and prayed in this manner, the more I realized my total dependence on God. I need Him for everything and in everyway.

He is my Father.
His will is the answer in any situation.
He will give me the resources to fulfill His will.
He will lead me in the way I should go.
He will deliver me.
He will protect me.
He owns the Kingdom, the Power and the Glory forever.

This prayer states clearly what God will do. It states His expectations of me. It is a simple prayer that is easy to understand and replicate. It is not complicated and shows how effortless it can be to talk to God.

I wrote this prayer book to encourage you, to convey the meditations of your heart to God.

Prayer is a powerful tool and we can and should just pray.

His love and mine

Day One

Surrender

Father, I surrender my heart to You, and choose to follow Your path for every area of my life.

Scripture: Job 11:13 and 15
13. Surrender your heart to God; turn to Him in prayer,
15. Then you won't be ashamed; you will be confident and fearless.

Jeremiah 10:23
Lord, I know that people's lives are not their own; it is not for them to direct their own steps.

Word
The meaningful journey of my life did not begin until I chose Jesus as my Lord and Savior. A purposeful life needs direction from the Author who defined the purpose. God who created all things; is the most qualified to direct our paths. He has already chosen you, surrender your heart to Him and turn to God in prayer.

Prayer
Dear God, You know the beginning and the end at the same time. You are the most qualified to direct my path. I choose Your path for my life today. I surrender my will to Yours. I yield to You for guidance in earthly and heavenly matters. The Bible says, I did not choose You, but You chose me. I acknowledge You as my Lord and Savior. I surrender my heart to You and turn every area of my life to You. I am able to love You because You first loved me. Help me be steadfast as You are steadfast. Help me cling to You and focus only on You. If I do not choose You, I have made a choice to be led by uncertainty. If I do not surrender my heart to You, I have by default, surrendered to the ruler of the world. It is not my will to be led by Satan. The Bible says; there is only one God. I choose to follow You **alone.** Your will for my life, will be done on earth as it is in heaven. I will forever yield my heart and mind to your direction. Your purpose for my life will be accomplished daily. Help me delight myself in Your great goodness. **Father, I surrender my heart to You and choose to follow Your path for every area of my life, in Jesus mighty name. Amen.**

Day Two

Your Path for Me

Father, may You matter more to me than "Isaac." Help me stay committed to Your path for me.

Scripture: Proverbs 16:9
A man's heart plans his way but the Lord directs his steps

Genesis 22: 1-19
2. Then He said, "Take now your son, your only son Isaac, whom you love, and go to the land of Moriah, and offer him there as a burnt offering on one of the mountains of which I shall tell you."

3. So Abraham rose early in the morning and saddled his donkey, and took two of his young men with him, and Isaac his son; and he split the wood for the burnt offering, and arose and went to the place of which God had told him.

Word
The demands and challenges of the world could distract us from seeking Gods face, if we focus more on the problem than we do on the solution. In the book of Genesis, Abraham was willing to obey God and sacrifice his only son, until God provided a ram in the bush. When we surrender to God, it cannot be done in half measures. When God directs our paths, we must be willing to do **whatever** He asks us to do, no matter the **cost.**

Prayer
Dear God, Help me be as obedient and committed to Your words, as Abraham. I will not be disobedient; neither will I rebel against You. May you matter more to me than "Isaac." Help me cling more to You, the Blessor, than I do to the blessings. Help me stay in communion with You. Help me learn Your ways and apply Your teachings in decision-making. Help me stay committed to You in my mind and heart. I pray that my thoughts are pure and holy, and reflective of Your hand upon my life. Help me translate my commitment into actions that are pleasing to You. Direct my every step and give me discernment to know when something looks and sounds good, but is not of You. Guide me through the precious Holy Spirit. Do not let me waiver in my faith. Give me light on the road I should travel. Let all the plans of my heart align with Your plans for me. **Father, may You matter more to me than "Isaac." Help me stay committed to Your path for me, in Jesus mighty name. Amen.**

Day Three

Your Image of Me

Father, help me accept Your image of me. Help me see myself as You see me.

Scripture: Genesis 1:26-28

26. And God said, "Let Us make man in Our own image, after Our likeness: and let them have dominion over the fish of the sea, and over the fowl of the air, and over the cattle, and over every creeping thing that creepeth upon the earth.

27. So God created mankind in His own image, in the image of God created them; Male and female He created them

Word

No image of me that is contrary to my creators' image is worthy of acknowledgement. The only image of you that is worth exploring, cultivating and accepting, is the image of your maker. The manufacturers description of their product is the only description that matters. Anyone is free to interpret the product in his or her own words, but calling the sky, earth doesn't make it so. Therefore, only your makers' description of you matters. What does God say about you? He calls me the apple of His eye and says that I was made in His own image. I believe Him and so should you.

Prayer

Dear God, You created and formed me in Your own image. The Bible says that You knew me before I was in my mother's womb. You are the Alpha and Omega, the beginning and the end. You are all things and You know all things. You blessed me to be fruitful and multiply in Your image. The way You see me, is the only vision of me worth knowing and accepting. It is the only image of me that truly exists. Help me be mindful of Your wonders and remind me daily that I am one of Your miracles. Father, save me from the enemy's web of lies. Do not let me internalize any opinion of me that doesn't align with Your view. Do not let me give in to illusions and unbelief. Once You have said it and settled it, who am I to try and undo it? Help me know Your voice that I may only hear what You say about me. I will not be a slave to a worldly image that will not bring You glory. I will not be lured by worldly accolades that are meaningless to You. I will not believe nor take to heart, anything that has not proceeded from You. I will remind myself daily, through Your word, to see myself as You see me. **Father, help me accept Your image of me. Help me see myself as You see me, in Jesus mighty name. Amen**

Day Four

My Father's Business

Father, as You predestined Jesus, and set him on His life's mission, help me be about My Father's business.

Scripture: Luke 2:49 and 50
49. And He said to them, "Why did you seek Me? Did you not know that I MUST be about My Father's business?"

50. And Jesus increased in wisdom and stature, and in favor with God and men.

Word
Nothing I do on this earth matters if it doesn't matter to God. If you want to increase in wisdom, stature, and in favor with God and man, the only way, is to be about your Heavenly Father's business. Education and work matters, but only if they enable us thrive in our God given purpose. In order to be about our Father's business, we need to know what "business," He has called us to. What business has God entrusted to you?

Prayer
Dear God, You sent Jesus to be an example on earth. His footsteps are to lead us directly to You. He is a living testament of a life spent in service to You and mankind. A life scarified for You, counts in Your kingdom. Dear Jesus, help me follow Your path to the Father. Help me to take up my cross and follow in Your obedient footsteps to the Father. I pray to receive all that is pre-ordained for me. No more trial and error, no more wishing and hoping I am in the right field. No more guessing games, wondering if the things I do, glorify God. Father, I want to know beyond the shadow of a doubt, that whatever my hands find to do, are the things You want me to do. I pray that absolute obedience to Your word is my only focus. I pray that You continue to remind me that the outcome is up to You and obedience is up to me. **Father, as You predestined Jesus, and set him on His life's mission, help me be about My Father's business.**

Day Five

Good Success

Father, help me observe to do according to Your word, so my way may be prosperous and I will have good success.

Scripture: Joshua 1:8
This book of the Law shall not depart from your mouth, but you shall meditate in it day and night, that you may observe to do according to all that is written in it. For then you will make your way prosperous, and then you will have good success.

Word
Gods' definition of success is the only one worth living for and celebrating. God said He would give us "good success." It will come directly from Him as a result of our total obedience. It does not matter if we get honor and accolades from man if God does not recognize why we are being honored. Good success doesn't mean we get what we want. It means we get what God gives, and His gifts are always profitable to our Souls.

Prayer
Dear God, I do not want to be trapped by baseless and empty accolades of this world. I do not want to inherit the wind. Give me Cisterns already dug, Vineyards, Olive groves and Fruit Trees in abundance. Help me to be wise of heart. I will not trouble my own house. I will not be a servant to the wise of heart. Help me remember You are the only one who yields the increase. Any increase that does not come from You is emptiness. I will not be enthralled by the misgivings of worldly success. Neither will I be lured by "success" gained from the misery of others. Earthly gains from disobedience to Your word will not be my portion. Help me know when to rejoice because the accomplishment is a completion of what You have pre-destined. Help me know when the celebration is baseless and will not bring You glory. I do not want to hope and long for anything that is not in Your will for my life. **Father, help me observe to do according to Your word, so my way may be prosperous and I will have good success, in Jesus mighty name. Amen.**

Day six

Secret Sin

Father, deliver me from "secret" sin.

Scripture: Psalm 90:8
You have set our iniquities before you, our secret sins in the light of your presence.

Job 11:14
And give up your sins – even those you do in secret.

Nehemiah 13:14
Do not let me return to my bondage

Word
The Bible says that there is nothing hidden that will not be revealed and no one can hide anything from a God who sees all things and knows all things. Sin saps spiritual power and separates us from God. ***All sin brings separation.*** It doesn't matter if it is done in the open or hidden. Sin is sin. Nothing we do in darkness stays in darkness forever. God has seen it, and that is all that matters. God takes our sin away and forgives us when we face the truth about our failings.

Prayer
Dear God, put an end to my foolishness. Nothing can be hidden from You. Help me understand that anything I do in secret is already revealed to You. I may be able to hide it from mankind, but You see all things and cannot be mocked. You know my failings. I do not want to continue in "secret" sin. I ask You to break the yoke of bondage that brings me back to lick my vomit like a dog. Lord Jesus, deliver me from falling for anything that Your sacrifice overcame. Help me surrender any unwilling part of my life that wants to remain in bondage and chooses to go against Gods commands. I pray that the gift to choose freely will not cause me to turn my back on You. How can I let my light shine for the world to see if I am hiding in darkness because of un-confessed sin? There are no secrets between You and me. **Father, deliver me from "secret" sin in Jesus mighty name. Amen.**

Day Seven

Forgive like You

Father, teach me to forgive like You.

Scripture: Mathew 6:12
Forgive us our debts as we forgive our debtors

Mathew 6:15
But if you do not forgive men their trespasses, neither will your Father forgive your trespasses.

Word
Forgiveness is one of the most important tools that enables us live abundant lives. We short-change ourselves when we do not forgive. We forget that scripture says: "forgive us as we forgive others." If we do not forgive, our Father will not forgive us. Why hold on to un-forgiveness when the only person you are hurting is yourself? Release others from their offenses, if you want to be released from yours.

Prayer
Dear God, You have been so good to me. You have not counted my sins against me. You forgive me daily. I would not be able to withstand the consequences of my disobedience. I pray that You give me a heart like Yours and show me how to share Your grace with others. We all need grace and cannot live in this sinful world without it. Deliver me from hypocrisy. I cannot continue to seek Your face and Your hand for anything I do not intend to share with my fellow man. All good things come from You. Everything You give to one of us is for all of us. Teach me to forgive. Help me show others how to extend forgiveness. We cannot begrudge our brothers and be free of grudges. A life of abundance cannot be achieved if we are hard of heart. You bless us so that we can be a blessing. You forgive us so that we can forgive others. Do not allow me to harden my neck, but help me heed all Your commandments. **Father, teach me to forgive like You, in Jesus mighty name. Amen.**

Day Eight

Brothers' Keeper

Father, help me to be my brother's keeper.

Scripture: Romans 14:19
Therefore, let us pursue the things, which make for peace and the things by which one may edify another.

Word
When we understand godly love and the price that Christ paid on the cross, we see how to be our brother's keeper. We are instructed to love our neighbors as ourselves. We are to consider our neighbor's needs whether they are present or not. Relationships can be difficult and cause us to ignore this mandate. But God did not ask, He instructed and we ought to obey.

Prayer
Dear God, help me understand what it means to be my brothers keeper. Every good thing I wish for myself, I want for my fellow man. I pray that I will be in service to the needs of others and not just my own. Jesus was a perfect example of how we should relate with others. I pray You will help me adopt his example. I want to be kind and considerate to others in my mind, heart, and actions. The Bible reminds us "as a man thinketh in his heart, so he is." Therefore as we think about others in our mind, so they are. I will see my brothers as God sees them. I will look upon you as God looks upon you. I pray that God will not permit me stand in judgment of anyone. I will be more compassionate of the plight of others. You will keep me from mob mentality and from joining the masses in condemnation of others. I pray that You will help me join with You instead. I will lift my brother and edify him. We will glorify Your holy name together. I will not join those who do not stand with You. **Father, help me be my brothers keeper, in Jesus mighty name. Amen.**

Day Nine

Parents

Father, help me honor my parents and release them from shackles of blame.

Scripture: Ephesians 6:1-3
1. Children, obey your parents in the Lord, for this is right.

2. Honor your father and mother, which is the first commandment **_with promise._**

3. That it may be well with you and you may live long on the earth.

Word
Some parents make mistakes, which negatively affect their children. A child of such parents might feel justified to dishonor them. However, the Bible tells us "vengeance is the Lords." Any parent who has been unjust to their children will have to deal with the consequences. The choices you make are your responsibility. It is better to obey God no matter how difficult it may be or how justified we feel.

Prayer
Dear God, I release my parents and myself from the hurt and pain of the past. I thank You for their lives and for bringing me into the world through them. I thank You for reminding me of Your commandment about my parents. Thank You for direction on how to treat my parents. You said, I should honor my father and mother, but You also tell me why: "that my days may be long on the earth." Whenever I pray for long life to see my children's children, it is because I have first honored my parents. They are worthy of forgiveness for any sins they committed against me, as I am worthy of Your forgiveness. I will not go against Your word. You instruct me to honor them not only because they deserve it, but also because You have commanded it. I trust You to guide me to speak life unto them. I pray that You will help me stop blaming them for the way my life turns out. As an adult, I am free to choose and any decision I have made is mine, not theirs. Yield my heart to You and soften my heart towards my parents. **Father, help me honor my parents and release them from shackles of blame, in Jesus mighty name, Amen.**

Day Ten

Siblings and Extended Family

Father, help me choose to love my siblings and extended family.

Scripture: 1 Peter 3:8
Finally, all of you be of one mind, having compassion for one another, love as brothers, be tenderhearted, and be courteous

Word:
We did not choose our siblings and extended family. God chose them and put them in our lives for a reason. Sometimes, it might be difficult to see why these particular people are family, but we know that God doesn't make mistakes. He chose our family, and when we choose to love them, we yield to His will. God works everything out for our good.

Prayer:
Dear God, You are all seeing and all knowing and You chose my earthly family: Father, Mother, Brothers, Sisters, and extended family. I pray that You help me embrace Your will. I pray that you show me how to obey You so I can get along with them. Help me extend love and forgiveness to all family members. I honor You when I honor them. I pray that Your grace and loving kindness will lead us in our thinking. I pray our hearts would be tender, compassionate, understanding and non-judgmental towards one another. We are not the master builder. You are aware of the areas in our lives that lack Your perfect will. You are the only one qualified to judge. All You require from us is love for others, and ourselves but more importantly, that we love as You first loved us. **Father, help me choose to love my siblings and extended family, in Jesus mighty name, Amen.**

Day Eleven

Friends

Father, Choose my Friends.

Scripture: Proverbs 27:17
Iron sharpeneth iron and so does the countenance of friends

Proverbs 14:23
In labor there is profit, but idle chatter leads only to poverty.

Word
The Bible says; the company we keep contributes to the quality of our lives. We want to be surrounded by people who keep us grounded in the word of God and His expectations. We ought to be a source of encouragement and support to our friends. True friends build each other up and hold themselves accountable. If you are my friend, I will not leave you or forsake you, by Gods grace.

Prayer
Dear God, help me choose a team of people who will aid the fulfillment of Your purpose for my life. Do not let me invest in any relationship, if You are not at the center. Surround me with people who want to obey You and who will not entice me to disobey You. You are love, I am love and all my friends are love. No one in my life will have an agenda different from Yours. You word says idle chatter leads only to poverty. Deliver me from idle chatter and let me only labor for profit. Help me be a friend who enriches the lives of others. Help me be iron, which sharpens the countenance of everyone around me. Give me friends who are just like You. Let my life read like a living Bible. Let my character and actions align with Yours. Help me cover a transgression, because I seek Your love and direction in all matters. Do not let me repeat a matter and separate friends. Let me dine on herbs where love is instead of eating a fatted calf with hatred. Let my friendships thrive on Your word. **Father, choose my friends, in Jesus mighty name, Amen.**

Day Twelve

Career

Father, choose my career and make Your choice plain for me to see and follow.

Scripture: Ephesians 2:10
For we are His workmanship, created in Christ Jesus for good works, which God prepared before hand that we should walk in them.

Psalm 139:16
Your eyes saw my substance being yet unformed, and in Your book they all were written. The days fashioned for me when as yet there were none of them.

Word
We were created for good works, which God prepared before hand. We are predestined with a mission, like Jesus. If God chooses our career, He will choose our coworkers, staff, and business partners. Even if there is a Judas amongst them, God orchestrated everything, and everyone would be there to fulfill destiny. The best field to work and build our career in, is the field God calls our greener pasture

Prayer
Dear God, Your word says that I am Your workmanship created for good works. You said I should bring my first fruits into Your storehouse and watch You bless the works of my hands. Father, make Your way plain before my face so the career I choose is my green pasture. Let the connection between what You need me to do and what You want me to accomplish, be clear and strong. Let me wake up every morning on a mission. I do not want to struggle for work that brings me joy, fulfillment and abundance. I do not want to settle in a "successful" career that is outside Your plan. I do not want to partner with anyone who is not in business with You. My work environment will be a reflection of You. The Holy Spirit will guide my co-workers and staff. I pray my work inspires and fuels me with passion, to serve You and others. Any work I do will be about Your kingdom agenda. My career goals will be at the center of Your will. You are a steadfast guide and I will trust You with every decision I make, whether it is popular or not. You are the only one who can define success and Your definition will guide my steps and how I record my accomplishments. My career will give me opportunities to answer the great commission, and lead others to You. **Father Choose my career and make Your choice plain for me to see and follow, in Jesus mighty name, Amen.**

Day Thirteen

Teachers

Father, may my teachers hearts be ruled by You.

Scripture: 1 Corinthians 11:1
Imitate me just as I also imitate Christ

Proverbs 14:24
The crown of the wise is their riches, but the foolishness of fools is folly.

Word
Teachers provide education in formal and informal settings. They are knowledgeable and wise, but we must not imitate without understanding. We have to know who directs the paths of those we wish to follow. We do not want to be led by people who are unable to follow principles and values of good moral character. We must not be led by shameful gain as described in 1 Peter 5:1-5. We, who are to be taught by our elders in Christ, must also be humble and willing to learn.

Prayer:
Dear God, give me teachers who love and serve you from their heart. Do not let me be at the mercy of Teachers who do not know You. Save me from leaders who refuse to accept they have lost their way. Do not let me fall prey to teachers who use their positions to mislead souls. Save me from those who care more about their earthly positions than they do about You. Stir me away from blind Teachers who refuse to repent. Make me teachable, humble and ready for Your steady hand of correction. Help me love instruction and knowledge, **so I know Your voice for myself.** Help me recognize Your voice in others. Guide my family and loved ones away from "spiritual teachers" who do not serve You. Keep us away from anyone who wants to influence us to move from Your side. Let me be wise, so the way of life winds upward for me. **Father, may my teachers hearts be ruled by You, in Jesus mighty name, Amen.**

Day Fourteen

Spouse

Father, Choose my Spouse.

Scripture: Genesis 2:8
The Lord God planted a garden eastward in Eden, and there He put the man whom He had formed

Genesis 2:18
And the Lord God said, it is not good that man should be alone; I will make him a helper comparable to him.

Word
Let it be settled once and for all, that the helper, God created is the one suitable for the man. A woman, who wishes to be married, ought to trust the creator to reveal the man He created her for.

Prayer
Dear God, I pray for revelation knowledge and understanding of Your order. You know everything about me. If I desire to be married, it is because You have already created the most suitable mate for me. My relationship with You will reveal and confirm my spouse. I want to be complete and whole as a single person. I want to be focused on building a solid relationship with You. Help me use this time to discover who I am in You. Help me say yes to Your YES and no to Your NO. Reveal the filters that matter to You. Do not let me create filters that lead to vanity. Help me understand that marriage is an institution established by You, for the furtherance of Your kingdom. Let my heart only yearn for the mate You have preordained for me. Help me wait on You. Help me see why I am suitable for my spouse and let our union bless generations. **Father, choose my Spouse, in Jesus mighty name, Amen.**

Day Fifteen

Children

Father, I thank You for the gift of Children. Show me how to raise my children.

Scripture: Proverbs 22:6
Train up a child in the way he should go, and when he is old he will not depart from it.

Psalm 127:3
Children are a heritage from the Lord; the fruit of the womb is a reward.

Word
ALL children are a heritage from the Lord. No matter how a child comes into our lives, whether by birth, adoption, or through our work; all children are equal in Gods eyes. We must first be trained up by the word of God so we are equipped with the right tools to raise them and not lead them astray.

Prayer:
Dear God, I thank You for the fruit of the womb. I know that all children under my care are my children. It doesn't matter how they come into my life. I am responsible for all the children left in my care at any given point in time. I pray that You will teach me what to teach them. Help me understand that I am not a superior being to these children. I am a custodian of Your creations. It is an honor and privilege to serve them. I want to obey Your will and desire for each of them. Show me the right way. Help me train them up. Help me raise them up. I cannot teach what I do not know. Let everything I teach them be visible in my actions. Children will often do what they see. I pray that my lifestyle will lead them to You. Help me submit to Your teachings. Help me live according to Your word. Let me be a guiding light. **Father, I thank You for the gift of children. Show me how to raise my children in Jesus mighty name, Amen.**

Day Sixteen

Like Joseph

Father, be with me like you were with Joseph, in the pit, prison and palace.

Scripture: Genesis 39:21
But the Lord was with Joseph and showed him mercy

Genesis 39:2
The Lord was with Joseph

Genesis 39:5
So it was from the time that he had made him overseer of his house and all that he had, that the Lord blessed the Egyptian's house for Joseph's sake; and the blessing of the Lord was on all that he had in the house and in the field.

Word
God was with Joseph and his story ended the way it began; he fulfilled his destiny. Sometimes we just want to know how the story ends. It is nice to know the end in the beginning, so when the storms come, we are able to withstand and overcome them. We must encourage ourselves in the Lord and cultivate His presence for divine order.

Prayer
Dear God, I pray that You would be with me like You were with Joseph. Walk with me through every life stage. You were with him in all places through out his life. When he was naïve and lacked wisdom, You protected him. Be with me when I am naïve and unwise. Be with me in the pit, in prison and in the palace. Be with me throughout my life's journey. Do not let my challenges seem small before You. Watch over me when others connive and seek my destruction. Elevate me in every area of my life. Give me wisdom that confounds the wise. Give me strategies that will save a kingdom. Give me a pure mind and pure heart. Help me seek the good in others. Let Your blessing upon me, bless others in their households and in the field. I want to be acceptable in Your sight. Help me express everything that you have ordained for me. I know that my actions are not always pleasing to You. I pray that You will show me mercy like Joseph. **Father, be with me like You were with Joseph, in the pit, prison and palace, in Jesus mighty name, Amen.**

Day Seventeen

My Place

Father, help my find my place in ministry.

Scripture: Ephesians 4:11-12
11. And He Himself gave some to be apostles, some prophets, some evangelists, and some pastors and teachers

12. for the equipping of the saints for the work of ministry for the edifying of the Body of Christ

Word
There is a particular place in ministry where gifts, abilities, talents and passion collide. God has given us a unique capacity to serve others. Our uniqueness helps us function in ministry. God will lead you to available tools to help find your place in ministry. Serve in the place where you gifts, abilities, talents and passion collide.

Prayer
Dear God, You made me for a purpose. I have been supernaturally fashioned to serve You and mankind. You equipped me with spiritual gifts, talents, passion and abilities. There is a particular environment in which the combination of all that I am will flourish. Do not let me lose the zeal to serve You. Do not let me find my place in the wrong environment. Let me flourish in "good soil." Help me find my place in service. Give me a Moses assignment. You gave him all the necessary resources, to complete his assignments. You told him: where to go, who to talk to, what to say, who would help him, and what to expect. He did not need to gather locust or buy red dye for the Nile. Father, I ask for the provision of Moses. Give me clear direction of what I am supposed to do. Lead me to my assignment and help me arrive in the land of promise. **Father, help my find my place in ministry, in Jesus mighty name, Amen.**

Day Eighteen

Money

Father, help me be a master to money.

Scripture: Mathew 6:24
No one can serve two masters, for either he will hate the one and love the other, or else he will be loyal to the one and despise the other. You cannot serve God and mammon (money).

Word
"The Love of money, (not money itself), is the root of all evil." We need provision to live and help the needy. When God blesses us, it is not for us alone. We have to be faithful custodians of the money and resources in our possession.

Prayer:
Dear God, give me freedom from want and limitations. Help me see money as a manifestation of Your provision in my life. I am a child of the most High God. I will not be a servant to money. Let the currency in my hand be relevant in all nations. I will never be broke. I will not love money more than I love You. I am a custodian of the wealth you place in my hands. I will be faithful and bless others. I take dominion over money. A lack of money will not dictate my movement or control my decision-making. I will further Your kingdom agenda. You are my source and I will obey Your every command. You will direct my spending and sowing. I will not steal and I will not borrow. I will not beg for my birthright. Money will not be a barrier between You and me. I declare that I am rich beyond measure. I will bring glory to Your name. Poverty and suffering will not prevail in my home or in the lives of my extended family or anyone who comes in contact with us. I will be a cheerful giver. Help me pay my bills cheerfully and on time. The money You give to me will be spent responsibly and not ostentatiously. My wealth will change generations for good and prevent lack in every area of my life. Help me set my heart on You and not on riches. **Father, help me be a master to money, in Jesus mighty name, Amen.**

Day Nineteen

The Actual Church

Father, lead me to a place of worship where the people (Church) who come to the Church (the building) reflect Your love and light.

Scripture: Acts 20:28
Therefore take heed to yourselves and to all the flock, among which the Holy Spirit has made you overseers, to shepherd the church of which He purchased with His own blood.

Word
Many Churches are stuck on: religion, programs, events, their own agenda and worldly entertainment. We are gradually losing focus of Gods kingdom agenda. We, the people, are the Church. We must fulfill the great commission, to make disciples of all nations. There are some worship centers that are focused on building the people and not the building. God will lead us to them.

Prayer
Dear God, I am part of Your Church. The buildings where Christians gather are not the Church. We, Your children, are Your Church. Let my heart towards You and my fellow man make me worthy to enter into Your presence and spiritual gatherings. Do not let me mock the Church by reducing it to calendar events. Show me how to be a true worshiper. Help me win souls for Your kingdom and build others up to the glory of Your name. Help me carry Your presence everywhere I go. You are in worship building, because You are in the people who go in there. You are in our midst when we gather in Your name. Do not let me find rest in a house of worship You do not recognize. Place me with a body of believers who are heaven bound. **Father, lead me to a place of worship where the people (Church) who come to the Church (the building) reflect Your love and light, in Jesus mighty name, Amen.**

Day Twenty

Broken Heart

Father, heal my broken heart.

Scripture: Psalm 34:18
The Lord is near to those who have a broken heart, and saves such as have a contrite spirit.

Psalm 147:3
He heals the brokenhearted and binds up their wounds.

Word
We should be compassionate, loving and kind. We never really know what a person is going through or what they have had to endure in life. We walk around daily looking well; but underneath the surface, we are asking God to heal our hearts and take the constant pain away.

Prayer
Dear God, heal my broken heart, spirit, and wings. Heal me from wounds that are reopened daily, in a world devoid of compassion and understanding. Help me hold my peace with people who are insensitive. Do not let me take offense when someone unknowingly reopens old wounds. I will lay down my cross so You can heal the pain of my past. Guide my interactions and keep them free of prejudice and malice. Help me offer love and not judgment. Help me build healthy relationships. Help me recognize that my spirit is already whole. I will not keep silent in despair. I will come to You first, when I feel lost and broken. Help me trust You to make all my crooked ways straight. I know You are the Lover of my Soul and You will not leave me in a broken state. You will mold and fill me with Your goodness and mercy, all the days of my life. **Father, heal my broken heart, in Jesus mighty name, Amen.**

Day Twenty-One

Good Works

Father, let my good works speak for me in my absence.

Scripture: Nehemiah 5:19
Remember me, my God, for good, according to all that I have done for this people.

Genesis 40:5 to Genesis 41:38
40:12 Now there was a young Hebrew man with us there, a servant of the captain of the guard. And we told him and he interpreted our dreams for us

Word
Be good to others at all times. God is always watching. Joseph was forgotten in prison. The Butler and Baker did not remember him after they were set free. But two years later, Pharaoh had a dream and the Butler remembered Joseph. He was released, he interpreted Pharaoh's dream and was elevated.

Prayer
Dear God, I know that You are faithful to keep good accounts. I know that I am not perfect. I have disappointed You in many ways. Father, You know my heart. I do not wish evil on anyone. I want the best for my fellow man. I want a heart like Yours. Help me continue to obey Your word. Help me make the right choices and take action that is pleasing to You. Help me continue to be the light in darkness. I will not offer a stone when my sister asks for bread. I will pray and continue to take action to meet the needs of others. You are a just God. Let Your forgiveness and grace cover my failings. Let my good works speak for me in my absence. Wherever my name is mentioned, raise a witness who will testify of the good that I have done. **Father, let my good works speak for me in my absence, in Jesus mighty name, Amen.**

Day Twenty-Two

Hopelessness

Father, deliver me from hopelessness and unfruitful labor.

Scripture: Luke 5:4-7

4. When He had stopped speaking, He said to Simon. "Launch out into the deep and let down your nets for a catch."

5. But Simon answered and said to Him, "Master, we have toiled all night and caught nothing; nevertheless at Your word I will let down the net."

6. And when they had done this, they caught a great number of fish, and their net was breaking.

7. So they signaled to their partners in the other boat to come and help them. And they came and filled both the boats.

Word
No one wants to toil all night, and go home broken and empty handed. We want to be rewarded for our labor. We want to see the fruits of our labor. We commit to doing the work because we believe we will receive and get to enjoy the rewards.

Prayer
Dear God, do not let me go home empty handed. I do not want to be a stranger to the covenants of promise. Deliver me from hopelessness. You did not let Peter turn back and dock his boat without a catch. You will not let me go home empty handed. Those who watched me toil all night will not be able to mock me. No one will refer to me as "fatherless." They will see the evidence of Your provision and multiplication. You will show up on time to rescue me. My "net" will not come up empty. You will tell me the precise location to cast my "net into the deep." Like Peter, my net will be filled, and everyone around me will be blessed from the overflow. Our testimony of such an abundant blessing will make us fishers of men. I will put my hope and trust in You. I will testify of Your goodness forever. **Father, deliver me from hopelessness and unfruitful labor, in Jesus mighty name, Amen.**

Day Twenty-Three

Darkness

Father, do not let me remain in darkness.

Scripture: Luke 1:78-79
78. Through the tender mercy of our God, with which the Dayspring from on high has visited us;

79. To give light to those who sit in darkness and the shadow of death, to guide our feet into the way of peace

Word
I do not want to catch a glimpse of Gods goodness and not partake in it. When we lack understanding in spiritual matters, we deprive ourselves of clarity and Gods perfect plan.

Prayer
Dear God, keep me in my right mind. Establish positive thoughts. Do not let me remain in darkness in a room filled with Your light. Help me send out goodwill to others, that I may receive goodwill. Father, do not let me sink into a deep sleep by the open gates, which lead to my land of promise. Save me from spiritual blindness. Let Your eternal light lead me away from eternal darkness and damnation. Do not let me succumb to discouragement and impatience. I will not try to produce the promises You alone can bring to pass. Help me trust You more. Help me embrace Your sufficient grace. Keep me in perfect peace. **Father, do not let me remain in darkness, in Jesus mighty name, Amen.**

Day Twenty-Four

My Heart

Father, supply the desires of my heart, as I delight myself in You.

Scripture: Psalm 37:4
Delight yourself in the Lord, and **He will give you** the desires of your heart.

Word
I can interpret the scripture above, to mean that God will give me whatever I desire in my heart. I believe it means; if I first delight myself in the Lord, He will supply the desires of my heart because He will cause me to desire His will.

Prayer
Dear God, Deliver me from trying to get You, to conform to my will, knowingly or unknowingly. Help me seek You first. I want to discover Your mind on a matter before I make a decision. Save me from myself. Save me from the desire to do what I know, instead of what You know. Help me understand and follow Your perfect order. I will find satisfaction in seeking Your face and serving You. I will set my mind on anything that brings You glory. Your will is my utmost desire. The Bible says, "Your word will not return to You void." You promised to give me the desires of my heart, if I delight myself in You. I adore You. You are my most perfect gift. It is my hearts desire to love and obey You. I do not want anything that doesn't come from You. Thank You for delivering me from wanting anything outside Your will. **Father, supply the desires of my heart, as I delight myself in You, in Jesus mighty name, Amen.**

Day Twenty-Five

My Calling

Father, help me understand there is no competition when I function in my calling.

Scripture: Philippians 2:3-4

3. Let nothing be done through selfish ambition or conceit, but in lowliness of mind let each esteem others better than himself.

4. Let each of you look out not only for his own interests, but also for the interests of others.

Word

It is Gods, design for us to be purpose filled and unique. Competition and the idea to be 1st, 2nd and 3rd, is the way of the world. Competition can be a great tool, when used to build people up and inspire them to greatness. When it makes others feel, less than, marginalized, or demoralized, it has crossed boundaries and lost its usefulness.

Prayer

Dear God, You did not create me to be in competition for my destiny. Help me understand that my position is not to be first, second or third, but to be all that You created me to be. **Do not let me run a race for a perishable crown.** I was created to serve and praise You. I pray You will help me focus on my calling and not on worldly goals. Help me covert you more. I do not want to yearn for things that "show" the world I am doing well, but "tell" you that my heart is far from you. Show me the ways of Your Kingdom. I do not want the ways of the world to be my goal in life. I do not want to be first in the things of the world, last in spiritual matters and exempt from the book of life. Help me see competition for what it is. Do not let me leave Your side for the recognition of others. My victory is in You. **Father, help me understand there is no competition when I function in my calling, in Jesus mighty name, Amen.**

Day Twenty-Six

My Home

Father, do not let my home be a war zone, give us perfect understanding.

Scripture: Isaiah 32:18
My people will dwell in a peaceful habitation. In secure dwellings, and in quiet resting places.

John 10:10
The thief does not come except to steal, and to kill, and to destroy. I have come that they may have life, and that they may have it more abundantly.

Word
My home should be a place of peace and harmony, but sometimes, that is not the case. Misunderstanding and miscommunication that would easily be amicably resolved at work or among friends, turns the home into a war zone. Satan hates peace and harmony and he is our number one enemy. Next time your home feels like a war zone, take your focus off the disagreement, turn to God and through Him, defeat the enemy who wants to steal, kill and destroy. Resolve all issues amicably, and trust God for peace and harmony.

Prayer
Dear God, You came from heaven to earth to show me the way to an abundant life. I thank You for the gift of life and a place to call home. Sometimes, life doesn't feel like a gift and the home front feels like a war zone. I know that Satan is not resting and is constantly trying to derail me. Do not let me fall prey to any of his schemes. Show me a way of escape. Help me put on Your full armor against the fiery darts of the enemy. Deliver me from battles with loved ones. Help us see each other through Your love. Give all the inhabitants of my home the gift of clear and effective communication. Let us speak less and listen more, with a heart of understanding and the Spirit of unity. Calm the raging sea, smooth any rough edges and let Your peace abide in my home. **Father, do not let my home be a war zone, give us perfect understanding, in Jesus mighty name. Amen.**

Day Twenty-Seven

Go with Me

Father, go with me wherever I go.

Scripture: Mathew 1:23
Behold, the virgin shall be with child, and bear a Son, and they shall call His name Immanuel, which is translated, God with us.

Word
There are days I feel like the struggle to maintain my sanity eludes me. Sometimes I sink into a desperate state and wish that life would be easier. I realize in those moments, I have forgotten God and forgotten who I am in Him. We should not be so consumed with our experiences that we forget Emmanuel; God is always with us.

Prayer
Dear God, go with me wherever I go. Do not let me dishonor You with my thoughts, words or actions. Be with me in my thoughts. Do not let me dwell on things I cannot control. Be in the meditations of my heart. Save me from fruitless endeavors. Keep me from empty promises. Be with me in my feelings. Do not let inconsistent feelings control me. Lead me with Your steady hand. Help me be emotionally stable. Be in the words I speak. Help me use language that would inspire, motivate and affirm others and myself. Do not let me ruin anyone's reputation. Be in everything I do. Let my actions resemble You. Help me move closer to You. Help me lead others to You. Do not let me turn anyone away from Your presence. You are my sustenance and deliverer, my everlasting hope and shield, the lifter of my head and circumstances. I will continue to abide in You and You in me. **Father, go with me wherever I go, in Jesus mighty name, Amen.**

Day Twenty-Eight

Dreams

Father, help me dream like Joseph.

Scripture: Genesis 37:5 and 9
5. Now Joseph had a dream, and he told it to his brothers

9. then he dreamed still another dream and told it to his brothers

Genesis 43:26
And when Joseph came home, they brought him the present, which was in their hand into the house, and bowed down before him to the earth

Word
The Bible says we should write the vision and make it plain. Before we write the vision, we must first be able to see it in our minds eye. What we write is what we visualize. It is important to see clearly, but it is more important to see what God sees for us. God's vision for us is the vision we want to write and run to accomplish.

Prayer
Dear God, I want to dream like Joseph. I want vivid dreams from You that come to pass. Give me dreams about my destiny that will propel me and keep me focused.
Let Your divine design take over my mind and visualization. Do not let me be content with building a bungalow when I should be building a palace. I want my dreams and visions to be guided by what You see. I do not want to guess that I heard from You or saw a vision, which did not originate from You. The same way Joseph was emphatic about what he saw in His dream, help me hold fast to whatever You reveal to me. Joseph was a dreamer but his dreams came to pass. I do not want to be a dreamer with no manifestation of the dream. If you allow me to see the vision, and enable me to write it down, help me bring it to pass in my lifetime. Let Your good spirit instruct me in the way that I should go. **Father, help me dream like Joseph, in Jesus name, Amen.**

Day Twenty-Nine

Perilous Pestilence

Father, deliver me from the snare of the fowler and the perilous pestilence.

Scripture: Psalm 91: 3
Surely He shall deliver me from the snare of the fowler and the perilous pestilence

Word
The snare of the fowler is a trap. Perilous pestilence is a devastating epidemic. Why would I need to be delivered from a trap and devastating epidemic? Who seeks my destruction and who is close enough to set a trap in wait for me? The thought of needing to be protected from anyone who seeks to harm me could be debilitating, if I didn't know God is always on my side. I am thankful for Gods promise of protection. Be encouraged, God is on your side.

Prayer
Dear God, I thank You for Your presence in my life which gives me daily confidence. I know that anyone who waits for my destruction is already defeated. Wickedness exists in the world, in high and low places, and Your word even mentions some in "heavenly places." Help me yield to the prompting and warnings of the Holy Spirit. When Your angels bare me up, do not let me rescue myself from their embrace. I thank You for shoring me up on all sides so that evil cannot penetrate my heart, loved ones and home. Subdue those who stand against me in judgment. The Bible says; a thousand may fall at my side and ten thousand at my right hand, but it will not come near me. You are the great deliver. There are times I think the storms of life will literally swallow me up, but Your roar and stance keep me safe. I do not take Your protection for granted. **Father, deliver me from the snare of the fowler and the perilous pestilence, in Jesus mighty name, Amen.**

Day Thirty

Abundance

Father, help me hear the sound of an abundance of rain and give me the grace to obey You promptly.

Scripture: 1 Kings 18:41
Then Elijah said to Ahab, "Go up, eat and drink; for there is the sound of abundance of rain."

Word
Sometimes, we sabotage our journey by going against the grain to interrupt what would have been a natural occurrence. In an attempt to speed up the results of our expectations, we muddy the waters and prolong the process. Patience is not only a virtue, but also, a necessity for greatness. In the above referenced scripture, Ahab had no idea what was about to happen, but Elijah did. What would have happened if Ahab had ignored the instruction he was given? There is a very thin line between obedience and disobedience. "Go up, eat and drink." My response: Yes Lord!

Prayer:
Dear God, do not let me stand in opposition of my greatness. Help me hear Your instructions clearly, **the first time.** Give me the grace to obey You promptly. The signs of the times are not a direct reflection of what You are doing. By Your command, a Seven-year famine could come to an end in an instant. Help me accept that I cannot understand everything about You. I am not the master planner. My plans and expectations may be good but not expedient. Help me identify Your sheep that know Your voice. Do not let me turn a deaf ear to Your Prophets. Disobedience and stubbornness will not hijack Your plans for me. I will not be led down a slippery slope, where I cannot be rescued. Do not let me interfere with Your orchestration. Do not give me access to prolong any process You have ended. Give me a double portion of patience. Let me answer Your instructions with a resounding; yes Lord! **Father, help me hear the sound of an abundance of rain and give me the grace to obey You promptly, in Jesus mighty name, Amen.**

Day Thirty-One

Just Reward

Father, let "You will reap your just reward," be a prayer for me and not a curse. Complete, establish, secure, strengthen and settle me.

Scripture: Luke 23:41
And we indeed justly, for we receive the due reward of our deeds; but this man has done nothing wrong

1 Peter 5
And after you have suffered a little while, the God of all grace who imparts all blessing and favor, who has called you to His own, eternal glory in Christ Jesus, will Himself complete and make you what you ought to be, establish and ground you securely, and strengthen, and settle you.

Word
We should expect the consequences and rewards of our actions. Whatever we give or put out into the world, we must be ready to receive. It is imperative to be intentional about our actions and contributions to the welfare of the world we live in. Let our suffering be for good.

Prayer
Dear God, I do not want to take and not give. You have blessed me tremendously and You continue to bless me daily. Let everything I sow on this earth and in anyone I am privileged to influence, be to the glory of Your name and not mine. I have confidence in You to complete what You have started in my life. I pray that You will establish me, secure all that concerns me, strengthen my resolve to sow and reap justly, and settle me. I will not run from pillar to post. I will not seek redemption from mere mortals. I will not lose my way in You. I will not miss the mark. I will make heaven. My name will be in the book of life. I will not prevent anyone from making heaven. I will answer the call of the great commission and make disciples of all nations. I will share You with everyone I meet. I will share love through my thoughts, words and deeds. You will be for me an everlasting reward. My legacy will be in You and those I have led to You. My food will be to do Your will and finish the work. **Father, let "You will reap your just reward," be a prayer for me and not a curse. Complete, establish, secure, strengthen and settle me, in Jesus mighty name, Amen.**

Name of God

Maker of Heaven and Earth

Name of God

I AM that I AM

Name of God

Way Maker

Name of God

Everlasting Father

Name of God

Awesome Wonder

Name of God

Pillar that Holds my Life

Name of God

Alpha and Omega

Name of God

My Friend

Name of God

Lifter of my Head

Name of God

My Jubilee

Name of God

Lover of my Soul

Name of God

My Savior

Name of God

My Light

Name of God

Peace River

Name of God

Joy Giver

Name of God

My Redeemer

Name of God

Most High

Name of God

Emmanuel

Name of God

My Shepherd King

Name of God

Great Physician

Name of God

Wonderful Counselor

Name of God

My Helper

Name of God

My Fortress

Name of God

My Rock

Name of God

My Deliverer

Name of God

My Shield

Name of God

The Horn of my Salvation

FINAL NOTE: GIVE UP. GIVE IN, SURRENDER ALL, TO GOD ALMIGHTY

In the course of writing this prayer book, I have seen scales fall from my eyes, yokes removed, burdens lifted, and years of bondage come to an abrupt end.

May your lives be forever transformed, may your hearts remain open. May your life's journey be, simple and true to Gods perfect will. Amen

Be encouraged to live the life He gave you.

BeBe

Be who God created you to **Be**

Acknowledgements

I thank God for the ability to hear His voice. I do not take my relationship with Him lightly. He proves to me daily, that I am the apple of His eye. Thank you my forever-faithful Father.

I am eternally grateful to my parents, who raised me in love and sent me to All Souls Church, for Choir practice, where I encountered God and caught a glimpse of heaven.

In order not to leave any names out, I want to thank all of you, who have been on this journey with me. Each of you has been a blessing and my life would not be the same without the special experiences I share with you.

My FAB prayer partners, who encourage me to speak to my Father, lift me up and agree with me in prayer to fulfill Gods call on my life, I thank you for showing me what prayer warriors look like.

My writing partners on all my writing projects, especially Ndidi on this particular project, thank you for encouraging me to put my words on paper. We will not labor in vain.

Thank you ever so much. May God establish and consolidate you. Amen.

"Pray without ceasing," Pray!

If you would like to continue the prayer conversation with 'BeBe' Abolade, please reach out via Facebook or Twitter:

Facebook: BeBe Abolade
Twitter: @BeBe Abolade

www.ingramcontent.com/pod-product-compliance
Lightning Source LLC
Chambersburg PA
CBHW072022060426
42449CB00034B/1826